A CHRISTMAS COOK BOOK

RECIPES BY
JUNE DUTTON

ILLUSTRATIONS BY
BRUCE BUTTE

CONTENTS

CRANBERRY PUDDING, 42
CRANBERRY SNOW, 40
DATE PIE, 36
EGGNOG CAKE, 48
EGGNOG CREAM PUFFS, 46
EGGNOG PIE, 44
EGGNOG SAUCE, 47
FRUIT-NUT COOKIES, 32
GINGER-PEAR PIE
   À LA CRÈME, 50
LEMON REFRIGERATOR
   CAKE, 48
MINCEMEAT CRÊPES, 51
PFEFFERNÜSSE, 30
PIE CRUST, 40
WHISKEY PUDDING, 43
WINE ORANGES, 37

DRINKS

BRANDY EGGNOG, 60
CRANBERRY MIST, 59
CRANBERRY RUM PUNCH, 60
HOT CRANBERRY PUNCH, 55
HOT BUTTERED RUM, 58
HOT MILK PUNCH, 58

MULLED WINE, 54
SPICED TEA, 54

ENTREES

ACORN SQUASH, STUFFED, 76
BAKED HAM WITH
   CRANBERRY GLAZE, 68
BAKED HAM WITH RAISIN
   SAUCE, 69
BEEF, KIDNEY & OYSTER
   PIE, 74
CINNAMON PANCAKES OR
   WAFFLES WITH PECAN
   BUTTER, 86
CRANBERRY FRENCH
   TOAST, 87
CRANBERRY OMELETTE, 82
CRANBERRY PANCAKES OR
   WAFFLES, 85
CURRANT STUFFING, 65
CURRIED SAUSAGE, 80
EGGS ON ANCHOVY TOAST, 80
FINNAN HADDIE, 84
HAM & CIDER BUFFET
   MOLD, 77

LAMB, CROWN ROAST, 68
RICE STUFFING, 64
ROAST BEEF & YORKSHIRE
   PUDDING, 67
ROAST CHICKEN &
   CRANBERRY STUFFING, 66
ROAST GOOSE, 64
ROAST LOIN OF PORK
   WITH PRUNES, 71
ROAST TURKEY, 62
SAUSAGE-CHESTNUT
   STUFFING, 63
SAUSAGE-CURRY SHORTCAKE, 78
SCALLOPED CHEESE, 79
SCRAMBLED EGGS, 81
SHRIMP SUPPER, 78
TONGUE VINAIGRETTE, 70
TURKEY GRAVY, 62
TURKEY PIE, 72

SIDE DISHES

APPLE BALLS, 88
APPLES, GLAZED, 89
CHESTNUTS, GLAZED, 90
CRANBERRY-APRICOT
   RELISH, 92

CRANBERRY-MINT RELISH, 93
GOOSEBERRY SAUCE, 94
MINT-ONION RELISH, 88
MUSHROOM RELISH, 94
PICKLED GRAPES, 95
PICKLED PRUNES, 95
RED & GREEN PEPPER
   RELISH, 96

SALADS

AVOCADO SALAD & TOMATO
   SOUP DRESSING, 97
BUFFET FISH SALAD, 98
CAULIFLOWER SLAW, 98
GREEN BEAN & BEET SALAD &
   PARMESAN DRESSING, 100
MUSHROOM SALAD, 101
RADISH SALAD, 99

SOUPS

BAKED POTATO SOUP, 108
CARROT VICHYSSOISE, 102
CLEAR BORSCHT, 104
OYSTER CHOWDER, 105

VEGETABLES

POTTED TONGUE

1 corned beef tongue
1 large onion
6 or 8 peppercorns
1 stick butter
1 tablespoon horseradish
1 teaspoon minced parsley

Put whole tongue into pan with cold water to cover. Add onion and peppercorns. Bring to boil, simmer until tender. Skin tongue and grind ½ to ¾ pound using finest grinder disc. Melt butter and add horseradish and parsley. Mix in ground tongue. Transfer to small covered crock or dish. Refrigerate until butter has hardened. Serve on rounds of rye bread or toast. Remainder of tongue may be sliced and frozen for future use.

CAVIAR DIP

2 tablespoons onion, minced
½ cup heavy cream, whipped
3 tablespoons caviar
3 hard-cooked egg yolks, grated fine
Lemon slices
Buttered toast

Fold onion into whipped cream. When thoroughly mixed, carefully fold in caviar. Spoon into serving bowl and cover with grated egg yolk. Garnish with lemon slices. Serve with toast.

BUTTERED TOAST:

Remove crusts from thin slices of firm white bread. Brush slices generously with melted butter and toast under the broiler. Cut in bite-size pieces.

STUFFED MUSHROOMS

½ pound small fresh mushrooms
⅔ cup cream cheese
1 teaspoon drained prepared horseradish
1 teaspoon minced dill pickle
1 teaspoon minced capers
 Pimento

Remove stems and wipe mushrooms clean with damp cloth. Cream the cheese with horseradish, pickle and capers. Fill mushrooms with cheese mixture and top with a small piece of pimento. Chill before serving. Cheese may be used to stuff celery also.

CLAMS OREGANO

2 dozen cherrystone clams
1 stick butter
2 tablespoons minced parsley
2 cloves garlic, minced
1 teaspoon dried oregano
½ cup bread crumbs
   Parmesan cheese, finely grated

Wash clams thoroughly so that all sand is removed. Steam clams until shells open (about 20 minutes). Meanwhile, melt butter and mix with parsley, garlic, oregano and bread crumbs. Remove clams from shells. Reserve liquid in steamer. Separate shell halves and set aside. Chop clams coarsely and stir into butter mixture. Fill clam shells (you will need about 18) and place in baking dish. Moisten each with ½ teaspoon clam broth. Sprinkle clams with grated Parmesan and broil until lightly browned. Serve immediately. Serve with lemon wedges.

SPINACH PIE

1 9–inch pastry shell (½ of pie crust
    recipe page 40)

1½ cups chopped cooked spinach

4 tablespoons butter
    Salt and pepper to taste

1 cup ricotta cheese

3 eggs, lightly beaten

½ cup freshly-grated Parmesan cheese

½ cup heavy cream
    Freshly-grated nutmeg to taste

Bake pastry shell for 15 minutes in 425° oven. Prick bottom with a fork before baking. Do not allow pastry to brown. Cook spinach with ½ teaspoon salt. Drain well. Mix with butter, salt and pepper. Combine ricotta, beaten eggs, Parmesan, cream and nutmeg. Add spinach, and spoon into pastry shell. Bake at 375° for 30 minutes or until crust is brown and spinach mixture is set. Test by inserting a knife in pie.

CLAM PIE

1 9-inch pastry shell (½ pie crust
   recipe page 40)
3 slices bacon, cut fine
1 medium onion, chopped fine
6 tablespoons minced parsley
1 can (7-oz.) minced clams
3 eggs, lightly beaten
⅔ cup cream
   Salt and pepper to taste

Bake pastry shell for 15 minutes in 425° oven. Prick bottom with a fork before baking. Do not allow pastry to brown. Set aside to cool. Sauté bacon. Add onion when bacon begins to get crisp. Cook until bacon is done and onions transparent. Drain and combine with parsley and clams. Beat eggs, add cream, salt and pepper. Add clam mixture to egg mixture and pour into pastry shell. Bake at 375° for about 30 minutes or until crust is brown and filling is set. Test by inserting a knife in center of pie.

HERB CUCUMBERS

1 large cucumber
2 tablespoons sour cream
1½ teaspoons vinegar
½ teaspoon sugar
1 teaspoon minced chives

1 teaspoon minced parsley
1 teaspoon minced fresh dill
   or ¼ teaspoon dried dill weed
Salt and cracked pepper to taste

Peel cucumber and slice very thin. Mix all other ingredients together and pour over cucumbers. Chill.

SEAFOOD COCKTAIL

½ pound cooked shrimp, crab,
   lobster or a combination
½ cup cocktail sauce
½ cup chopped celery
½ cup chopped cucumber

2 tablespoons chopped
   bell pepper
1 scallion, minced
2 teaspoons lemon juice
   Horseradish to taste (optional)

Combine all ingredients. Chill. Serve on shredded lettuce with avocado garnish or in cocktail cups.

PICKLED FISH

2 pounds salmon, center cut or
    2 pounds of filets
8 peppercorns
1 large bay leaf
1 teaspoon salt
½ cup onion rings
½ lemon, sliced
½ pound medium uncooked shrimp

Put salmon into a cooking pan with water to cover. Add spices, onion and lemon. Bring to a boil. Add washed shrimp. Cover and simmer for 5 minutes. Drain. Break salmon into bite-size pieces and alternate layers of fish, shrimp and sliced onion in a serving dish. Marinate with:

1½ cups white vinegar
6 tablespoons sugar
6 whole allspice

Combine ingredients and bring to a boil. Be sure sugar is dissolved. Pour over the fish. Cover and allow to stand overnight or longer.

COUNTRY PÂTÉ

Thickly sliced lean bacon to line
terrine or other baking dish.

1 pound ground veal
1 pound ground lean pork
½ pound ground calf liver
¼ pound diced slab bacon
2 large cloves garlic, minced
1 egg, beaten
1 teaspoon salt
½ teaspoon freshly cracked pepper
½ teaspoon allspice
1 teaspoon thyme
¼ cup coarsely chopped pistachio nuts

Preheat oven to 325°. Line baking dish with bacon. Using your hands, mix all other ingredients together. Fill bacon-lined dish with meat mixture, forming rounded top. Place several slices of bacon on top. Cover, using aluminum foil if dish has no cover, and bake for 1 hour. Remove cover or foil and bake 1 hour longer. Remove pâté from oven and allow to stand ½ hour. Put a light weight on top and allow to stand until completely cool. Refrigerate. Serve with crusty French bread.

TOASTED FILBERTS

1 stick butter
2 cups shelled filberts (hazelnuts)
1-2 tablespoons salt

Melt butter in a skillet and add nuts. Cook nuts, stirring, until golden brown. Remove pan from heat and continue to stir nuts for several minutes. Sprinkle with salt to taste. Cool and serve.

WALNUT-BACON WRAPS

Bacon slices
Walnut halves

Cut bacon slices into thirds and fry over low heat until translucent. Drain on paper towel. Wrap each piece around walnut half and fasten with toothpick. Broil on a rack about 3 inches under preheated broiler until bacon is crisp. Drain on paper towel. Serve immediately.

AVOCADO MOUSSE

3 envelopes unflavored gelatin
1 cup cold water
3 large ripe avocadoes, mashed
¼ cup fresh lemon juice
¾ cup sour cream
¾ cup mayonnaise
2 tablespoons grated onion
2 tablespoons minced parsley
2 tablespoons chopped pimento
  (optional)
⅛ teaspoon pepper
1 teaspoon salt

In a saucepan soak gelatin in the cold water. Stir mixture over low heat to dissolve gelatin. Place in refrigerator until consistency of un-beaten egg white. Watch it carefully or it will get too hard.

Puree or mash avocadoes with lemon juice. Combine with remaining ingredients. Fold in gelatin. Spoon into a 5½ cup mold rinsed with cold water. Cover with plastic wrap and refrigerate 3 hours or until set. Serve on buffet or as first course.

FRUIT CAKE BREAD

1½ cups milk
2½ envelopes dry yeast
1½ cups sugar
1½ sticks butter, melted
½ teaspoon salt
3 eggs, beaten
5–7 cups flour
¼ cup chopped candied orange rind
¼ cup chopped candied pineapple
¼ cup chopped candied cherries
¼ cup chopped candied citron
½ cup dark raisins
½ cup white raisins
1 cup chopped mixed almonds and pecans
¼ cup brandy

Scald milk and then let it cool to lukewarm. Dissolve yeast in milk. Add sugar, butter and salt. Add well-beaten eggs and about 3 cups of the flour, candied fruits, nuts and brandy. Add additional flour to make a soft dough. Turn out onto lightly floured board and knead until smooth. Cover and let rise in a warm place until double in bulk. Knead again and form 2 loaves. Place in loaf pans, brush with melted butter and let rise again to almost double in bulk. Bake in 350° oven 45 minutes to 1 hour or until toothpick inserted in center of loaf comes out clean.

STOLLEN
(Makes 3 Loaves)

2 cups milk
2 packages dry yeast
1 cup flour, sifted
1 pound soft butter
1 cup sugar
4 eggs
¼ cup rum

Grated rind of 1 lemon
Grated rind of 1 orange
1 cup chopped almonds
½ cup chopped candied ginger
2 cups raisins
1 cup chopped dates
7 cups flour, sifted

Scald milk and cool to lukewarm. Add yeast and 1 cup flour. Beat well, and set aside in warm place until mixture is light and slightly airy. Cream butter and sugar. Beat in eggs one at a time. Add yeast mixture, rum, grated lemon and orange, almonds, candied ginger, raisins, dates and 7 cups flour. Place dough on a lightly floured board and knead until smooth. Remove to a greased bowl, cover with a towel and allow to rise until double in bulk. Divide dough into 3 parts, roll out slightly, press down center with a rolling pin, brush with melted butter and fold over. Brush the top with melted butter and place loaves in buttered bread pans. Let rise until double in bulk. Place in preheated 350° oven and bake 45 minutes to 1 hour or until golden in color. Cool slightly and frost (page 23) if desired.

WHITE FROSTING:

2 cups confectioners' sugar
3 tablespoons hot cream
¼ teaspoon salt
2 teaspoons rum

Sift sugar and add gradually to hot cream, blending until creamy. Add salt and rum and blend. Makes 1 cup.

WHIPPED CREAM-HERB BISCUITS

2 cups flour
3 teaspoons baking powder
¾ teaspoon salt
½ teaspoon fines herbes
1 cup cream, whipped

Sift dry ingredients together into a mixing bowl. With a fork stir in whipped cream. On a lightly floured board knead the dough for about a minute and pat out to ¾-inch thickness. Cut with biscuit cutter and bake in 425° oven for 10 to 12 minutes. Serve hot.

SUGAR PLUM BREAD

2 (1 pound) cans purple plums, drained
1 stick butter
2 teaspoons baking soda
2 cups sifted flour
1 cup sugar
½ teaspoon salt
½ teaspoon cinnamon
¼ teaspoon cloves
1 cup seedless raisins
¾ cup chopped filberts

Preheat oven to 350°. Pit and mash plums. Combine plums and butter and heat slowly until butter is melted. Transfer to a large mixing bowl. Stir in baking soda. Allow mixture to cool until barely warm to the touch. Add all remaining ingredients to plums and mix well. Pour into a well-greased and floured bread pan. Bake for 70–80 minutes or until center is firm to the touch. Serve warm with whipped cream cheese.

ALMOND ROCA

½ pound butter
1 cup sugar
¾ cup coarsely chopped almonds
½ pound milk chocolate, melted
¾ cup coarsely chopped almonds,
      toasted

Butter a cookie sheet. Melt butter and bring to a slow boil. Add sugar and stir briskly over heat high enough to keep ingredients bubbling gently. When mixture has begun to blend (after 3 to 5 minutes) add ¾ cup chopped almonds. Continue to cook until mixture is thoroughly blended (2 or 3 minutes more). Never let the mixture become so hot that pan scorches or candy turns more than a pale buttery brown color. Candy is ready when a small bit dropped in cold water hardens immediately (hard ball reading on a candy thermometer). Spread ½-inch thick on cookie sheet. When cooled slightly, pour melted chocolate over the top. Sprinkle with ¾ cup toasted almonds. Cool thoroughly in refrigerator. Break into pieces and store in airtight container.

CANDY CANES

(Makes 10)

2 cups sugar
½ cup light corn syrup
½ cup water
¼ teaspoon cream of tartar
¾ teaspoon peppermint extract
¾–1 teaspoon red food coloring

In a saucepan combine sugar, corn syrup, water and cream of tartar. Stir until sugar dissolves. Continue to cook, without stirring, until candy thermometer registers 265°. Remove from stove and add extract. Divide mixture into 2 portions. Add red coloring to one. Cool to handling temperature. Butter your hands and pull each portion into lengths, then twist the red around the white. Cut into 8-inch lengths. Form canes.

LEMON TAFFY

2 cups sugar
2 tablespoons butter
¼ cup lemon juice

½ teaspoon fresh lemon rind, grated
¾ cup water

Stir all ingredients together and cook until mixture reaches 270° on the candy thermometer. Pour onto a buttered plate. When cool, pull taffy until it is snowy white. Pull into a long string and cut into one-inch lengths. Wrap in red and green Christmas foil.

COCOA BALLS

½ cup unsweetened cocoa
2 cups sifted powdered sugar
½ cup sweetened condensed milk
2 teaspoons brandy or vanilla
   Dash of salt
1 cup finely chopped walnuts

Knead together cocoa, sugar, milk, flavoring, salt and ½ of the nuts. Continue to work with hands until candy is smooth and well blended. Break off small bits and roll into balls. (Wet hands slightly for best results.) Then roll each ball in remaining nuts until covered. Place on a platter to dry. Makes 3 dozen or more.

PEANUT BRITTLE

  1 cup white corn syrup
  2 cups sugar
  ½ cup water
  2 cups raw Spanish peanuts
     (red skins)
1½ tablespoons butter
1½ teaspoons vanilla
  2 teaspoons soda

Put syrup, sugar and water into a heavy skillet and cook to the soft-ball stage (230°). Add peanuts. Stir and cook to the hard-crack stage (300°). Turn off heat. Stir in the butter, vanilla and soda. Pour the peanut brittle onto a greased surface (marble is best). Turn it at once and stretch it quickly until it is very thin. When cold break it into pieces.

CHOCOLATE SNOWBALLS

2 cups flour
1 teaspoon baking powder
½ teaspoon salt
¼ teaspoon baking soda
1½ sticks soft butter
¾ cup brown sugar, firmly packed
2 squares unsweetened chocolate,
    melted
1 egg
1 teaspoon vanilla
¼ cup milk
Powdered sugar

Combine first four ingredients in a sifter. Beat butter with brown sugar until fluffy. Beat in chocolate, egg, vanilla and milk. Sift in dry ingredients a little at a time. Mix into a stiff dough and chill until firm enough to roll by hand into small balls (1 teaspoon of dough per ball). Place 2 inches apart on cookie sheet and bake at 350° until tops are cracked, 8–10 minutes. Roll in powdered sugar while balls are still hot. Roll in sugar again after they cool.

PFEFFERNÜSSE

2 sticks soft butter
1½ cups sugar
3 eggs, beaten
5 cups flour
1 teaspoon salt
4 teaspoons baking powder
½ teaspoon cloves
½ teaspoon nutmeg
1 teaspoon cinnamon
½ teaspoon white pepper
1½ cups milk
½ cup water
1 cup chopped almonds
1 teaspoon anise seed

Cream butter and sugar until fluffy. Add eggs and mix well. Sift flour with next six ingredients. Stir into butter mixture alternately with milk and water. Add almonds and anise seed. Drop by teaspoon on buttered cookie sheet. Bake in 350° oven for 15 minutes. Remove and sprinkle with confectioners' sugar.

FRUIT-NUT COOKIES

1 cup soft butter
1½ cups brown sugar, firmly packed
3 eggs
3½ cups flour
¼ teaspoon cloves
½ teaspoon ginger
½ teaspoon nutmeg
1 teaspoon cinnamon
1 teaspoon soda
1¼ cups chopped dates
¾ cup chopped dried apricots
1 cup white raisins
1 cup mixed glazed fruit, chopped
1 cup chopped pecans

Preheat oven to 350°. Cream butter and brown sugar together until fluffy. Beat in eggs one at a time. Sift flour, spices and soda and add to butter mixture. Stir in fruits and nuts. Mix well. Drop the batter by spoonsful onto ungreased cookie sheet. Press cookies flat with wet fork. Bake about 15 minutes or until lightly browned.

CRANBERRY-CURRANT COOKIES

2½ cups currants
½ cup bourbon
½ stick soft butter
½ cup brown sugar, firmly packed
2 eggs
1½ cups flour
1½ teaspoons baking soda
1½ teaspoons cinnamon
½ teaspoon ginger
¼ teaspoon nutmeg
¼ teaspoon cloves
1 cup chopped pecans, toasted
1 cup coarsely chopped cranberries

Soak currants in bourbon for an hour. Cream butter and sugar together and add eggs. Mix well. Sift flour, soda and spices together and stir into batter. Add nuts, currants, bourbon and cranberries. Mix and drop by teaspoonsful on buttered cookie sheet. Bake at 325° until firm, about 15 minutes.

CHRISTMAS STARS

2 teaspoons sugar
1 egg
2 tablespoons butter, melted
¼ cup milk
1 teaspoon vanilla
¼ teaspoon salt
1½ cups flour
Corn oil
Powdered sugar

Beat sugar and egg together until fluffy. Beat in butter, milk, vanilla and salt. Add flour gradually until dough is thoroughly mixed. Roll out dough on a floured surface to ⅛ to ¼-inch thickness. Cut with star cookie cutter. Drop each star into hot (375°) corn oil. Turn stars once so that both sides will be golden brown. Drain on absorbent paper. Sprinkle with sifted powdered sugar. Store in airtight container.

BUTTER COOKIES

1 cup soft butter
½ cup sugar
2½ cups sifted flour

In mixer bowl cream butter and sugar until fluffy. With mixer on low speed, blend in flour. Roll dough into a ball and refrigerate for 1 hour. Preheat oven to 300°. Roll out dough ⅓-inch thick on lightly floured surface. Cut with Christmas cookie cutters. Decorate with cookie and cake decorations. Bake on ungreased cookie sheet 20–25 minutes.

ALMOND TILES

3 egg whites
½ cup sugar
2½ tablespoons flour
    Pinch of salt
½ stick of butter, melted
2 tablespoons whipping cream
½ cup slivered almonds

Beat egg whites and sugar together at high speed 2½ minutes. Add flour and salt and beat another minute. Stir in melted butter and cream. When well mixed, stir in almonds. On a 12×15-inch cookie sheet, spoon teaspoons of batter well apart from each other (about 8 cookies per sheet) and bake in a preheated 325° oven for about 10 minutes. Remove cookies from pan with pancake turner and shape over a rolling pin. Cool on a rack and store in covered container to keep crisp.

CHOCOLATE MOUSSE

6 squares semi-sweet chocolate
Dash of salt
3 tablespoons water
4 eggs, separated
2 teaspoons vanilla
1 cup whipping cream
2 teaspoons sugar

Combine first 3 ingredients in double boiler or a pan over very low heat. Stir until chocolate is melted. Beat egg yolks until thick and lemon colored. Gradually beat in chocolate. Stir vigorously or chocolate and egg mixture will lump. Add vanilla. Beat egg whites into soft peaks. Fold them into chocolate mixture. Whip half the cream with 1 teaspoon sugar and fold into the chocolate. Spoon the mousse into a serving dish or 8 individual portions. Chill for at least 2 hours. When ready to serve, beat the remaining cream with 1 teaspoon sugar and use as garnish.

DATE PIE

1 cup sliced dates
1 cup sugar
1 cup chopped pecans

1/4 teaspoon salt
2 egg yolks, beaten
1 teaspoon baking powder
2 tablespoons flour
2 egg whites, beaten

Thoroughly mix all ingredients except egg whites. Fold in egg whites and pour mixture into a greased 9-inch pie plate. Bake at 350° for 40 minutes. Serve warm with vanilla ice cream or whipped cream.

WINE ORANGES

8 large oranges
2/3 cup claret
1/3 cup sugar
1/4 teaspoon cinnamon
1/8 teaspoon ground cloves

Peel and section oranges. Remove all membranes. Place sections in serving dish. Heat wine, sugar, cinnamon and cloves until sugar is dissolved. Pour hot wine over orange sections and chill overnight. Serve with almond tiles (page 35).

CRANBERRY CHEESECAKE

12–16 graham crackers, crushed fine
7 tablespoons butter, melted
1 pound cream cheese (room
    temperature)
½ cup sugar
2 eggs
1 teaspoon vanilla

Preheat oven to 350°. Mix crushed graham crackers with melted butter and pat evenly over bottom of springform pan. Beat cheese, sugar, eggs and vanilla until smooth. Spread over cracker crumbs. Bake for 25 minutes. Remove from oven and spread with the following topping:

2 cups sour cream
2 tablespoons sugar
2 teaspoons vanilla

Mix ingredients well. Spread over cake and return to 350° oven for 5 minutes longer. Chill. Top with whole cranberry sauce before serving.

CRANBERRY SAUCE:

- 4 cups fresh cranberries
- 2 cups sugar
- 2 cups water

Wash and stem cranberries. Combine all ingredients and cook over high heat until berries begin to burst (about 5–8 minutes). Cool and spread over cheese cake.

CRANBERRY-APPLE PIE

- 1 double unbaked 9-inch pie crust (page 40)
- 1 cup cranberries, coarsely chopped
- ½ cup white raisins
- 2 cups chopped apples
- 1 cup sugar
- ¼ cup cranberry juice

Mix cranberries, raisins and apples with sugar. Spoon into bottom crust. Pour cranberry juice over the mixture. Add top crust making a few small slashes for escaping steam, and sprinkle lightly with sugar. Bake at 425° for 15 minutes. Lower heat to 350° and continue baking until crust is golden (about 45 minutes). Serve warm with vanilla ice cream or whipped cream.

PIE CRUST

2 cups flour   ⅔ to 1 cup vegetable shortening
⅓ teaspoon salt   Ice water

With your fingertips mix the flour, salt and shortening until the consistency of corn meal. The dough will be better blended by using your fingertips rather than cutting the shortening into the flour with a knife or pastry blender. Gradually add enough ice water to form dough into a ball. Roll out on floured surface with floured rolling pin. Makes one double 9-inch crust.

CRANBERRY SNOW

6 cups cranberry juice   ¾ cup water
1 cup sugar   3 tablespoons Cointreau
3 envelopes unflavored gelatin 1 cup heavy cream, whipped

Bring cranberry juice and sugar to a boil, stirring until sugar dissolves. Soften gelatin in water for 5 minutes, then stir into the hot juice until dissolved. Cool slightly and add Cointreau. Chill until mixture begins to set, then beat with a rotary beater until frothy. Pour into individual serving dishes and chill until set. Serve topped with whipped cream. Serves 8.

CRANBERRY PUDDING

1½ cups flour	½ cup light molasses
1 teaspoon soda	½ cup hot water
Pinch of salt	2 cups cranberries, washed, cut in half

Sift flour, soda and salt together. Stir molasses into hot water. Mix dry and liquid ingredients together. Add cranberries. Mix well. Fill greased mold two-thirds full. Cover tightly. (If mold has no cover, cover pudding with 1 layer of waxed paper and 1 layer of foil and secure tightly with string.) Steam in deep covered kettle on rack with water about half way up sides of mold for 1½ hours. Serve hot with sauce.

SAUCE:

½ cup butter
½ cup light cream
1 cup sugar
1 teaspoon vanilla, rum or brandy

Cook butter, sugar and cream about an hour in double boiler. Add vanilla. Serve hot on hot pudding.

WHISKEY PUDDING

9 ounces vanilla wafers
1 stick soft butter
1 cup sugar

4 eggs
1 cup chopped pecans
½ cup bourbon

Crush vanilla wafers fine in a plastic bag. Cream butter and sugar together until fluffy. Add eggs one at a time beating well after each addition. Add pecans and bourbon. Grease a one-quart baking dish and layer wafer crumbs and egg mixture, beginning and ending with layer of crumbs. Refrigerate at least 48 hours. Serve topped with whipped cream.

DESSERT CHERRY SAUCE

¾ cup sugar
1 tablespoon cornstarch
1 can (16-oz.) red, tart pie cherries
Kirsch to taste

Mix sugar and cornstarch. Put into saucepan. Add to undrained cherries and cook until cherry juice is thickened. Remove from stove, add Kirsch and serve warm over vanilla ice cream.

EGGNOG PIE

CRUST:

14 graham crackers, crushed fine
7 tablespoons butter, melted

Mix cracker crumbs and butter thoroughly and pat evenly over the bottom and sides of a 9-inch pie plate. Refrigerate.

FILLING:

1 tablespoon unflavored gelatin
¼ cup cold water
⅓ cup sugar
2 tablespoons cornstarch
⅛ teaspoon salt
2 cups commercial eggnog
1½ squares unsweetened chocolate, melted
1 teaspoon vanilla
2 tablespoons rum
1 cup heavy cream, whipped

Sprinkle gelatin over cold water to soften. Mix sugar, cornstarch and salt in a saucepan. Place over low heat and gradually (stirring constantly) add the eggnog. When mixture has thickened, remove from heat and stir in gelatin until dissolved. Divide filling in half. Add melted chocolate and vanilla to one half and set aside to cool. To remaining half add the rum and set aside to cool. When mixtures are cool, fold half of the whipped cream into each. Pour the rum flavored portion into the bottom of the chilled pie shell. Follow with the chocolate flavored portion and cover with topping.

TOPPING:

1 cup heavy cream, whipped
1/4 cup rum
1/4 cup confectioner's sugar
1/2 square unsweetened chocolate

Beat cream until slightly thick. Add rum and sugar and continue beating until thick enough to spread over top of pie. Sprinkle with grated chocolate. Refrigerate for at least 4 hours.

EGGNOG CREAM PUFFS

1 cup water
1 stick butter
1 cup flour
¼ teaspoon salt
4 eggs

Preheat oven to 450°. Heat water and butter in a medium-sized saucepan until mixture boils. Add flour and salt and beat vigorously over low heat until mixture comes away from the sides of the pan and forms a stiff ball. Remove from heat and add eggs, 1 at a time, beating thoroughly after each addition. Drop by teaspoon or tablespoon (depending on size desired) on a buttered baking sheet. For small puffs bake 15 minutes at 450° and then for 20 minutes at 325°. For larger puffs add 5 minutes to the 450° period. Fill with the following custard:

2 cups milk
¼ cup flour
¾ cup sugar
1 tablespoon butter
3 eggs, beaten
¼ teaspoon salt
¼ teaspoon nutmeg

1-2 tablespoons brandy
½ cup heavy cream, whipped

Scald milk in top of double boiler. Mix flour and sugar in a bowl and gradually pour the hot milk over them, stirring well. Return mixture to double boiler and cook, stirring constantly, until mixture thickens. Cover and continue cooking over low heat 15 minutes longer. Add butter. While stirring vigorously, add beaten eggs, salt and nutmeg. Stir and cook until eggs thicken. Cool and add brandy. Fold in whipped cream. Fill puffs with custard. Top with additional whipped cream and dash of cinnamon if desired or with eggnog sauce.

EGGNOG SAUCE

2 egg yolks
¼ cup powdered sugar
1 cup heavy cream
2 egg whites
¼ to ½ cup brandy

Cream egg yolks and powdered sugar. Whip cream and fold into eggs and sugar. Beat egg whites until stiff and fold into mixture. Stir in brandy. Serve as topping for eggnog cream puffs (page 46) or mincemeat crêpes.

EGGNOG CAKE

2 sticks soft butter
1 box superfine granulated sugar
6 eggs, separated
7-10 tablespoons bourbon
1 cup walnuts, chopped
2/3 pound lady fingers
1/2 cup heavy cream, whipped

Cream butter and sugar until fluffy. Beat egg yolks until thick. Slowly add bourbon to egg yolks and then combine with the butter mixture. Stir in nuts. Fold in stiffly beaten egg whites. In a serving dish place a layer of split lady fingers then a layer of eggnog mixture. Alternate the two, finishing with a layer of lady fingers. Refrigerate. Frost with whipped cream.

LEMON REFRIGERATOR CAKE

8 egg yolks, beaten lightly
3/4 cup sugar
Juice of 2 large lemons
Grated rind of 1 lemon
1 envelope unflavored gelatin
1/4 cup cold water
8 egg whites, beaten stiff
3/4 cup sugar
1 dozen lady fingers
Whipping cream

Cook egg yolks, ¾ cup sugar, lemon juice and rind in a double boiler until thickened. Dissolve gelatin in cold water and add to hot custard mixture. Beat egg whites with ¾ cup sugar. Mix custard into egg whites. Line a spring mold with lady fingers and fill with custard. Chill until set. Top with whipped cream and serve.

CRANBERRY COBBLER

    1 cup flour
    2 teaspoons baking powder
      Pinch of salt
    ¼ cup shortening
    ½ cup sugar
    ½ cup milk
    1 cup whole cranberry sauce
    1 cup cranberry juice
    ½ cup sugar
      Whipping cream

Sift flour, baking powder and salt together. Cream with shortening and add ½ cup sugar and milk. Spoon into a greased baking dish. Top with cranberry sauce, juice and remaining sugar. Bake at 375° for 50 to 60 minutes. Serve warm with whipped cream.

GINGER-PEAR PIE
À LA CRÈME

1 unbaked pie shell (9–inch), (½ pie
  crust recipe page 40)
2 (1–lb.) cans pear halves
¼ cup sifted flour
3 tablespoons brown sugar
½ teaspoon cinnamon
½ teaspoon nutmeg
2 tablespoons butter
2 teaspoons finely chopped candied ginger
2 eggs, beaten
½ cup sugar
¼ teaspoon salt
1 teaspoon grated lemon rind
1½ cups sour cream

Drain pears in sieve. With fingertips blend together flour, brown
sugar, cinnamon, nutmeg and butter until the consistency of coarse
crumbs. Mix in candied ginger and set aside. Combine eggs, sugar,
salt and sour cream. Pour half of cream mixture into pie shell. Arrange
pears in shell and cover with remaining cream. Top with brown sugar
mixture. Bake at 400° on rack just below oven center until filling is set
and crust is lightly browned (35–45 minutes). Cool before cutting.

MINCEMEAT CRÊPES

  1 cup sifted flour
  2 eggs
1½ cups milk
  2 tablespoons butter, melted
 ⅛ teaspoon salt
  1 teaspoon sugar
  1 tablespoon brandy
  1 pound mincemeat

Mix all ingredients except mincemeat and let stand overnight. Pour about 1½ tablespoons at a time into hot (lightly smoking) buttered skillet. Tip pan so that batter spreads very thin. Cook until top is dry. Turn and brown lightly on other side. Cool on aluminum foil. Spread each crêpe with 1 to 2 tablespoons warmed mincemeat. Roll and place in a lightly buttered baking dish. Warm crêpes 10 minutes in 325° oven. Serve topped with eggnog sauce (page 47). Makes about 2 dozen crêpes.

APPLE SNOW

8 large apples
¼ cup sugar
4 egg whites, beaten
½ teaspoon cinnamon
¼ teaspoon nutmeg
Dash of salt
½ cup sugar

Peel and core apples and place them in a baking pan just large enough to hold them close together. Sprinkle with ¼ cup sugar and bake in preheated 400° oven. When apples are soft, transfer to a blender or fine sieve and puree them. Beat egg whites with cinnamon, nutmeg and salt until they form soft peaks. Add sugar and beat until stiff. Fold in apple puree. Spoon into serving dish.

CHAMPAGNE SHERBET

2 tablespoons (2 envelopes)
    unflavored gelatin
½ cup cold water
½ cup sugar

1 bottle (fifth) champagne
2 egg whites

In a saucepan soften the gelatin in the cold water. Add sugar. Warm over low heat until gelatin and sugar are dissolved. Remove from stove. Add champagne. Pour into shallow pan and freeze until barely set. Beat egg whites and fold into the sherbet. Return to freezer and finish freezing.

CHERRY BAVARIAN CREAM

1 (16-oz.) can pitted sweet,
    dark cherries
1 tablespoon unflavored gelatin
1 cup whipping cream
2 tablespoons brandy
2 tablespoons sugar

Drain cherries and cut in half. Reserve juice in a saucepan. Sprinkle gelatin over surface of juice and allow to stand for 3 minutes. Warm juice over low heat until gelatin is dissolved. Cool. Whip cream with sugar and brandy until thick. Place pan with cherry juice in bowl of ice and beat juice until it begins to set. Fold in cream and cherries. Transfer to dessert mold and chill until well set. Serve with additional whipped cream if desired.

SPICED TEA

¾ cup sugar
½ cup cold water
Juice of 1 orange
Juice of 4 lemons
8 whole cloves
1 teaspoon cinnamon
5 cups boiling water
5 heaping teaspoons tea

Dissolve sugar in cold water before heating. Bring to a boil, remove from heat and add juices and spices. Pour 5 cups boiling water over the tea in a warm pot. Strain tea into fruit mixture. Serve immediately in punch cups. Garnish with lemon slices and cloves.

MULLED WINE

1 cup sugar
½ cup water
2 sticks cinnamon
½ lemon, sliced
2 dozen whole cloves
4 cups orange juice, heated

1 quart dry red wine
¾ cup white raisins

Combine sugar, water, cinnamon, lemon slices and cloves and boil for 5 minutes. Strain. Add hot orange juice. Heat wine and raisins to boiling point and add to hot juice mixture. Keep the mulled wine hot without boiling. Makes 2 quarts.

HOT CRANBERRY PUNCH

6 whole cloves
2 sticks cinnamon
4 whole cardamom pods, shelled
4 cups cranberry juice
1 cup light raisins
¼ cup sugar
2 cups claret wine

Place spices in a saucepan with 2 cups of the cranberry juice, raisins and sugar. Bring to a boil, lower heat and simmer (uncovered) for 10 minutes. Remove spices and cool punch. Before serving add remaining 2 cups cranberry juice and wine. Heat to almost boiling. Serve hot or over ice.

HOT MILK PUNCH

6 blanched almonds, pounded
    in a mortar
1 quart milk
1 teaspoon grated lemon rind
½ cup sugar
2 egg whites, lightly beaten
½ cup rum
1 cup brandy

Heat the milk, together with pounded almonds, lemon rind and sugar, to the scalding point. Remove from heat. Add egg whites, rum and brandy and beat lightly until mixture is frothy. Serve in punch cups.

HOT BUTTERED RUM

1 teaspoon maple sugar
¼ teaspoon minced lemon peel
3 pinches cinnamon
    Pinch of ground cloves

Pinch of nutmeg
1 jigger golden rum
Boiling water
1 teaspoon butter

For each individual serving: Scald a china mug. Put sugar, lemon peel and spices in it. Pour in rum. Add enough boiling water to fill mug. Drop in lump of butter.

CRANBERRY MIST

1½ cups cranberry juice
5 ounces vodka
2 teaspoons fresh lime juice
1 teaspoon sugar
1 egg white
Crushed ice

Combine all ingredients in a blender. Blend until foamy. If the drink stands and separates it can be re-blended a moment before serving.

BRANDY EGGNOG

1 teaspoon sugar
1 egg yolk
1½ ounces brandy
½ cup milk
   Ice cubes
   Nutmeg

Combine all ingredients in a shaker. Mix vigorously and strain into a 10-ounce highball glass. Dust with nutmeg.

CRANBERRY RUM PUNCH

½ cup fresh lemon juice
¼ cup sugar
1 cup cranberry juice
1 cup orange juice
1 cup strong tea
1 fifth white rum

Combine all ingredients and chill. Float ice cubes in punch after it is chilled.

ROAST TURKEY

Turkey
Butter
Salt and pepper

Wash turkey thoroughly inside and out and dry with paper towels. Stuff neck and body cavities loosely with sausage-chestnut dressing (page 63). Close openings with skewers or sew up with heavy thread. Place turkey, breast side up, in roaster or pan with cover. Butter breast, wings and legs. Sprinkle with salt and pepper. Roast at 325°, covered, until turkey is almost done. Baste with pan drippings every ½ hour. Long, slow cooking produces a moister more tender bird. Uncover roaster for last 45 minutes so that turkey browns nicely. Allow 25 minutes per pound for a turkey under 12 pounds and 20 minutes per pound for a larger bird.

TURKEY GRAVY

Giblets
1 medium onion
1 stalk celery
3 sprigs parsley
Salt and pepper to taste
Flour

Put giblets into a saucepan and cover with cold water (3 cups at least). Add onion, celery, parsley, salt and pepper. Cover and bring to a boil. Lower heat and simmer until gizzard is tender. Remove any excess fat from turkey drippings and add enough flour to make a thin paste (more flour if you like thick gravy). Blend flour and drippings thoroughly. Add liquid from giblets, stirring over medium heat so that gravy does not lump. If more liquid is required add water or chicken stock. Cook until gravy bubbles. Season to taste.

SAUSAGE-CHESTNUT STUFFING

(For A 12-pound Turkey)

¾ cup chopped, roasted chestnuts
1 pound highly seasoned (hot) pork
    sausage
2 apples, peeled and chopped
8 cups cubed white bread

Pierce chestnuts with a sharp knife and bake in 400° oven about ½ hour. Shell, peel and chop chestnuts. Sauté sausage in heavy skillet until almost done. Add apples and cook 1 minute longer. Add chestnuts and cubed bread. Mix well until bread has absorbed pork fat. Add salt or pepper if necessary. Stuff turkey cavities loosely.

ROAST GOOSE

1 12-pound goose
Salt

Wash goose well inside and out. Dry thoroughly with paper towels. Fill with rice stuffing (see below). Close neck and body cavities with skewers or sew together with heavy thread. Fasten wings to body and tie legs together. Prick surface with a sharp fork so that excess fat will cook out. Salt goose and place on rack in roasting pan. Roast in 325° oven until meat begins to pull away from leg bones. Allow 20–25 minutes per pound. Mix gravy according to directions for turkey gravy (page 62). Be sure to remove all excess fat.

RICE STUFFING

3 cups chicken stock
10-ozs. rice (wild and white mixed)
1½ cups coarsely chopped celery
1 cup sliced mushrooms
¾ cup chopped onion
¼ cup chopped parsley
½ stick butter
Salt and pepper to taste

Bring chicken stock to a boil. Add rice. Turn heat to low, cover pan and cook until stock is absorbed. Sauté celery, mushrooms, onions and parsley in butter. Mix with rice. Season to taste. Spoon into goose.

CURRANT STUFFING

8 cups cubed dried bread
1 10 oz. pkg. dried currants
1 cup port wine
1 cup boiling water
2 sticks butter, melted
1 large onion, chopped
3 large stalks celery, chopped
  Poultry seasoning to taste
  Salt and pepper to taste

Soak currants in wine for at least 2 hours. Mix currants and wine into bread. Add remaining ingredients and toss until thoroughly mixed. Will stuff a 12 pound turkery.

ROAST CHICKEN & CRANBERRY STUFFING

1 roasting chicken, 4 to 5 pounds
¾ cup raw cranberries, coarsely chopped
5 cups lightly toasted bread cubes
1 small onion, chopped fine
1 small clove garlic, minced
1 stick butter, melted
3 tablespoons brown sugar
½ cup raisins
1 teaspoon salt or to taste
1 teaspoon poultry seasoning
¼ teaspoon coarsely ground pepper

Wash chicken inside and out. Wipe dry and set aside. In a heavy skillet combine all other ingredients and cook over moderate heat for 5 minutes. Remove from heat and stuff the chicken loosely, both breast and neck cavities. Sew or skewer the openings. Place chicken on roasting rack, brush with ¼ cup melted butter and sprinkle with salt and pepper. Cook in moderate (350°) oven 2 hours. Baste frequently.

ROAST BEEF

Prime rib roast
Salt and pepper

Place meat in uncovered roasting pan on rack, fat side up. Roast in 350° oven until meat thermometer reads desired doneness (thermometer must not touch the bone). Allow 15–18 minutes per pound for medium rare meat. Salt and pepper meat after it has roasted for ½ hour. Serve with mushroom relish (page 94) or red and green pepper relish (page 96).

YORKSHIRE PUDDING:

⅞ cup flour
½ teaspoon salt
½ cup milk

2 eggs, beaten
½ cup water

Sift flour and salt into a bowl. Stir in milk. Add eggs and beat. Add water. Beat batter until large bubbles rise to the surface. Let stand 1 hour. While batter stands, make ready a hot oven-proof baking dish (10×10″) containing ¼ inch of hot beef drippings from the roast, or melted butter. Beat batter again and pour into pan. Bake at 350° for ½ hour until pudding is puffed up and brown.

CROWN ROAST OF LAMB

3 small racks of lamb
Salt
Pepper

Have butcher saw bones so that racks may be easily shaped into a crown. Remove excess fat, and trim meat off the tips of the ribs. Sprinkle with salt and pepper. Sew racks together to form crown. Protect rib tips from burning with aluminum foil. Roast in 325° oven for 1 hour or until done to taste. Remove to a platter and place a suitable sized warmed serving dish inside crown and fill with minted pureed peas (page 112).

BAKED HAM WITH CRANBERRY GLAZE

8–10 pound precooked ham
1 cup whole cranberry sauce
1 teaspoon prepared mustard
½ teaspoon cinnamon
½ teaspoon ginger
¼ teaspoon cloves
½ cup orange juice

Bake ham, covered, at 350° for 1 hour. Combine remaining ingredients and mix well. Remove cover from ham, drain any fat from pan and spread ham with glaze. Bake uncovered an additional ¾ to 1 hour basting at intervals.

BAKED HAM WITH RAISIN SAUCE

8–10 pound precooked ham
Whole cloves

Stud surface of ham with cloves. Bake ham, covered, at 350° for 1 hour. Remove cover and continue baking ¾ to 1 hour more. Slice and serve with hot raisin sauce.

RAISIN SAUCE:

1 cup claret
1 cup water
½ cup sugar
½ cup seedless raisins
1 teaspoon prepared mustard
¼ teaspoon ground cloves

Combine all ingredients and cook over moderate heat for 20 minutes.

TONGUE VINAIGRETTE

1 fresh beef tongue
1 bay leaf
10 peppercorns
1 tablespoon salt
1 large stalk celery with leaves, cut
    into quarters
1 small carrot, cut in half
1 large onion, quartered
3 or 4 sprigs parsley

Put tongue into cooking pot with cold water to cover. Add all other ingredients. Cover pot. Bring to a boil. Lower heat and simmer 2–3 hours until tongue is tender. While tongue is cooking prepare vinaigrette sauce:

1 small tomato, peeled and minced
2–3 tablespoons minced sour pickle
2 tablespoons minced parsley
2 large scallions with some tops, minced
1 tablespoon minced celery
1 small carrot, minced
6 tablespoons wine vinegar
3 tablespoons olive oil

6 tablespoons water
⅛ teaspoon sugar
  Salt and cracked pepper to taste

Combine all ingredients and allow to stand while tongue is cooking. Serve tongue sliced thin, either hot or cold, with sauce.

ROAST LOIN OF PORK WITH PRUNES

4–5 pound loin of pork
15 prunes, halved and pitted
1 cup prune juice
1 tablespoon prepared mustard
  Salt and pepper

Cut deep slashes into meat (about ¾ of an inch apart) and fill with prunes. Place meat in uncovered roasting pan on rack and bake in 325° oven for 1 hour. Increase temperature to 375° and roast for another hour or until meat thermometer registers 185°. During the final hour baste meat with prune juice to which mustard has been added. Season with salt and pepper.

TURKEY PIE

1 double unbaked 9-inch pie crust
   (page 40)
2 tablespoons butter
2 tablespoons flour
¾ cup chicken stock
⅓ cup half-and-half or milk
1 stalk celery, coarsely diced
2 to 3 cups of cooked cubed turkey
1 cup peas and carrots (frozen are fine)
¼ cup whole kernel corn
3 sliced mushrooms (optional)

Melt butter. Blend in flour. Add chicken stock gradually, cooking over low heat and stirring constantly so that sauce will be smooth. When thick stir in milk. Set aside. Cook celery in lightly salted water for 3 minutes. Drain. Layer turkey and vegetables in bottom pie crust. Pour sauce over and cover with top crust. (Make a few small slashes for escaping steam.) Bake 15 minutes at 450°. Reduce heat to 375° and bake 50 to 60 minutes longer.

BEEF, KIDNEY & OYSTER PIE

(Serves 12)

CRUST:

3½ cups flour
1 teaspoon salt
10 tablespoons chilled shortening
10 tablespoons chilled butter
2 teaspoons lemon juice
4 to 6 tablespoons ice water

PIE FILLING:

2 (10-oz.) jars oysters
2 veal kidneys
4 pounds beef stew meat
1 cup seasoned flour
12 tablespoons rendered
    beef suet
1½ cups chopped onions
1 pound mushrooms, sliced
2½ cups rich beef stock

2 teaspoons salt
2 teaspoons pepper
2 teaspoons crushed fresh
    rosemary
3 tablespoons chopped parsley
1 cup chopped parsley
1 egg yolk mixed with
    1 tablespoon milk

Put flour and salt into a bowl. Cut in shortening and butter until mixture resembles coarse gravel. Mix the lemon juice with the water and add enough water to form pastry into a soft dough. Roll into a ball, cover with waxed paper and chill.

Wash the kidneys, split them lengthwise, remove all the white fat and tubes and cut into thin slices. Cut the beef stew meat into 1½-inch-square pieces. Put seasoned flour into paper sack with the kidney and meat cubes and shake them until they are coated with flour.

Melt the suet in a heavy skillet, remove cracklings with slotted spoon and discard, then sauté the onions until transparent. Remove and reserve. Brown the beef and kidneys in the same pan. Remove and reserve. Add the mushrooms and sauté for a couple of minutes. Combine onions, meat, kidneys and mushrooms, add the beef broth, salt, pepper, rosemary and parsley, cover and simmer for 1¼ to 1½ hours or until meat is tender. Add oysters and liquor and simmer until edges of oysters curl. If sauce is too thin, thicken with 1 tablespoon of cornstarch mixed with 3 tablespoons of water.

Put the filling into a deep casserole or paella pan. Put a custard cup upside down in the center. (This will serve to hold up the crust.) Pour the sauce over the meat. Sprinkle the cup of parsley over the top. Roll out the crust and cover the pie, pinching the crust edges to seal. Make a few steam slits with the point of a paring knife. Brush with egg and milk mixture. Bake at 400° for 10 minutes, then at 350° for another 15 to 20 minutes.

STUFFED ACORN SQUASH

2 acorn squashes, cut in half lengthwise and seeded
1 pound pork sausage
1 tablespoon minced onion
2 tablespoons butter
2 tablespoons flour
½ cup beef broth
1 to 1¼ cups milk
1 package frozen spinach, defrosted and well
    drained or 1 cup fresh-cooked spinach
Freshly grated nutmeg to taste
Salt and pepper to taste

Sauté pork sausage and onions together. Drain on absorbent paper. Over medium heat melt butter and blend in flour. Add beef broth gradually, stirring constantly to keep sauce smooth. When thickened add milk. Stir in spinach, sausage, nutmeg, salt and pepper. Fill squash cavities. Place on baking sheet and bake in 375° oven until squash is tender, about 1 hour. Cover with foil for last ½ hour of baking.

HAM & CIDER BUFFET MOLD

1 cup white raisins
1 quart apple cider
¼ cup brown sugar
4 whole cloves
1 (1-inch) piece stick cinnamon
2 envelopes unflavored gelatin
3 tablespoons water
1 tablespoon lemon juice
½ teaspoon salt
  Dash of cayenne
2 cups cooked ham julienne
  Mayonnaise
  Beet juice

Soak raisins in cider until plump. Add brown sugar, cloves and cinnamon and gradually heat until first small bubbles appear. Meanwhile, soften gelatin in water and lemon juice. Remove cider mixture from heat and slowly stir in the softened gelatin. When dissolved, add salt and cayenne. Remove cloves and cinnamon stick. Place mixture in refrigerator. When it begins to thicken, gently stir in ham. Pour into a wet mold and chill until set. Serve with mayonnaise tinted with beet juice.

SAUSAGE-CURRY SHORTCAKE

    1 pound pork sausage (hot variety if
        preferred)
    1 cup thinly sliced onion
    1 small apple, diced
    3 tablespoons flour
  2-3 tablespoons curry powder or to taste
    2 cups milk
      Salt to taste
   10 hot baking powder biscuits, split in half

Sauté sausage until almost done. Add onion and apple. Cook until apple is barely tender. Combine flour and curry powder and mix into meat. Stir in milk and cook until thickened. Add salt. Serve over hot biscuits. Rice may be substituted for biscuits.

SHRIMP SUPPER

    1 clove garlic
   ¾ cup soft butter
    1 teaspoon salt
      Pinch of tarragon
      Pinch of marjoram

1 cup fine breadcrumbs
½ cup dry sherry
3 pounds shrimp, cooked and shelled

Mash garlic thoroughly and add to butter with salt, tarragon and marjoram. Cream until well blended, then add breadcrumbs and sherry. Mix well. In a large, buttered baking dish layer shrimp and breadcrumb mixture, sprinkling a layer of chopped parsley over each layer. Bake in a 400° oven for 20 minutes. Serve with green salad and sliced tomatoes.

SCALLOPED CHEESE

2 cups stale white bread, cubed
1¼ cups grated Cheddar cheese
2 eggs, beaten
1½ cups milk
    Salt and cracked pepper to taste
    Canned stewed tomatoes
4 slices crisp bacon, crumbled

Preheat oven to 375°. Mix bread and cheese in a baking dish. Beat eggs and combine with milk. Add salt and pepper and pour over bread and cheese. Bake 35 minutes or until cheese is melted and bubbly. Serve hot, topped with hot stewed tomatoes and crumbled bacon for breakfast or brunch.

EGGS ON ANCHOVY TOAST

6 slices bread, crusts removed
2 tablespoons butter
2 tablespoons anchovy paste
1 teaspoon English mustard
8 eggs, beaten
3 tablespoons heavy cream
1 tablespoon onion, minced

1 tablespoon green pepper, minced
Salt and pepper to taste
2½ tablespoons butter, melted in skillet
⅓ cup grated Cheddar cheese
Worcestershire sauce
Pimento strips

Toast bread lightly. Cream together 2 tablespoons butter, anchovy paste and mustard. Spread on toast and set aside to keep warm. Mix eggs, cream, onion, green pepper, salt and pepper and pour into skillet with melted butter. Remove from heat while eggs are still moist and slightly underdone. Spoon into mounds on anchovy toast. Sprinkle with grated cheese and a few drops of Worcestershire. Place under hot broiler until cheese melts. Garnish with pimento strips. Serve at once.

CURRIED SAUSAGE
(With Scrambled Eggs)

2 dozen small pork sausages
2 tablespoons flour

2 tablespoons curry powder
2 cups beer, heated to boiling point

Sauté sausages until done. Drain and reserve ¼ cup of the fat. In a saucepan mix fat with flour and curry. Stir for 3 minutes over very low heat. Gradually stir in the heated beer and allow mixture to simmer for 15 minutes. Add sausage, and salt if necessary. Serve over scrambled eggs.

SCRAMBLED EGGS

1 dozen eggs
5 tablespoons small curd cottage
    cheese with chives
1 tablespoon water
    Salt to taste
    Parsley sprigs
    Pimento strips

Beat eggs with cottage cheese, water and salt until fluffy. Melt butter in a large skillet and pour in eggs. Cook, stirring almost constantly with a fork over low to moderate heat until eggs are barely set. Garnish eggs and sausage with parsley sprigs and pimento strips.

CRANBERRY OMELETTE

(3 eggs per person)

1½ cups whole cranberry sauce
2 tablespoons orange juice
Rind of ½ an orange, grated
6 eggs
6 tablespoons milk
½ teaspoon salt
Butter
3 tablespoons whipping cream
Powdered sugar

Heat cranberry sauce with orange juice and rind. Set aside to stay warm. Thoroughly beat eggs, milk and salt together. Coat omelette pan, bottom and sides, with melted butter. Pour in the eggs and cook over low heat, moving the pan so that the omelette does not stick and browns evenly. When the eggs begin to set, pour cream over the top, spreading it evenly to the edges. When eggs are almost done, spread 3 tablespoons of the cranberries, leaving all the juice on the remaining berries, over the top of the omelette. Fold over and remove to a warm plate. Top with the rest of the cranberry mixture. Dust with powdered sugar.

FINNAN HADDIE WITH EGGS

2 pounds finnan haddie
Scalded milk to cover
1 stick butter, melted
⅓ cup flour
1½ cups chicken broth
1½ cups half and half
Salt and cracked pepper to taste
1 tablespoon parsley, minced
5 hard-cooked eggs, sliced in
    ½-inch rounds
Buttered toast

Place finnan haddie in greased baking dish and cover with scalded milk. Bake at 350° for 20 minutes. Meantime, combine butter and flour and cook over low heat for a few minutes. Gradually add broth and half and half, stirring constantly. When sauce begins to thicken continue cooking until quite thick and creamy. Bone finnan haddie and break into bite-size pieces. Add to cream sauce and simmer gently for several minutes. Season to taste. Add parsley and fold in eggs, being careful not to break them apart. Serve on buttered toast.

CRANBERRY PANCAKES OR WAFFLES

1 cup flour
2 tablespoons sugar
1 tablespoon baking powder
½ teaspoon salt
2 eggs, separated
2 tablespoons butter, melted
1 cup milk
1 cup coarsely chopped cranberries

Sift first four ingredients together. Add egg yolks to milk and beat. Mix in butter and cranberries. Beat egg whites until stiff and fold into batter. Spoon dollar-size pancakes onto hot griddle or pour batter onto greased waffle iron. Serve with generous amount of maple syrup, since berries are tart.

CINNAMON PANCAKES OR WAFFLES

Substitute 2½ teaspoons cinnamon and ⅓ cup finely chopped pecans for cranberries in recipe for cranberry pancakes (page 85). Serve with softened butter, to which you have added enough cinnamon to taste, and maple syrup or pecan butter.

PECAN BUTTER:

- 1 stick soft butter
- 1 cup brown sugar, firmly packed
- ⅓ cup milk
- 4 teaspoons brandy
- ⅛ teaspoon salt
- 1 cup finely chopped pecans, toasted

Beat butter until fluffy. Add brown sugar gradually. Mix in milk, brandy and salt. Beat for one minute. Add nuts. Spread on hot cinnamon pancakes or waffles.

CRANBERRY FRENCH TOAST

2 eggs, beaten
½ cup milk
Pinch of salt
12 slices thin white bread, crusts removed
1 cup jellied cranberry sauce
1 stick butter, melted

Mix eggs, milk and salt together. Spread 6 slices of bread with cranberry jelly. Cover with remaining bread slices. Dip sandwiches into egg mixture, turning so that both sides are soaked with egg. Fry in butter in a heavy skillet. Cover the skillet after both sides of the bread are browned so that the toast will be thoroughly cooked and light and fluffy. Top with melted butter and warm cranberry syrup.

CRANBERRY SYRUP:

2 teaspoons arrowroot
½ cup sugar
2 cups cranberry juice

Mix arrowroot and sugar thoroughly. Add to cranberry juice and heat until liquid thickens.

APPLE BALLS

1 cup sugar
1 cup water
4 cloves

Sliced rind of ½ lemon
1½ cups apple balls
Red or green food coloring

Combine sugar, water, cloves and lemon rind. Cook for several minutes until syrupy. Remove cloves and lemon rind. Add apple balls. (Apples should be peeled and cut with a melon ball cutter.) Add 1 or 2 drops food coloring. Cook until apples are tender. Chill and serve with roasted meats or poultry.

MINT-ONION RELISH

1 cup finely chopped onion
1 cup finely chopped fresh mint leaves
¼ cup finely chopped green pepper
2 tablespoons lemon juice
3 tablespoons salad oil
½ teaspoon sugar
Salt and cayenne pepper to taste

Mix all ingredients thoroughly. Chill overnight.

GLAZED APPLES

4 cups water

1½ cups sugar

Juice of one lemon

1 teaspoon cinnamon

6 drops red food coloring

4 medium-large Rome Beauty apples,
cut in half lengthwise, peeled
and cored

Mix all ingredients except apples in a saucepan and simmer for 5 minutes. Add apples and poach for 15 minutes turning them over once. Remove fruit from syrup and place (cutside down) in a flat baking dish. Over high heat, reduce syrup to ½ cup, pour over apples and bake in a 375° oven for 20 minutes. Turn apples over once and spoon syrup over them. Remove from oven. Turn apples once more and spoon syrup over them. Cool and use to garnish meat or fowl.

GLAZED CHESTNUTS

1 pound large chestnuts
Milk
1 tablespoon sugar
1¼ tablespoons butter
¼ cup butter
4 tablespoons sugar
1¼ tablespoons flour
1 tablespoon water

Make a cut in the flat side of each chestnut and bake them in a very hot oven 10 to 15 minutes or until shells and skins are easily removed. Simmer peeled chestnuts in milk to cover with 1 tablespoon sugar and 1¼ tablespoons butter, until barely tender. Drain well. Melt ¼ cup butter in a frying pan. Add 4 tablespoons sugar, and stir until golden brown. Add flour and water and bring to a boil, stirring constantly. Add chestnuts. Salt to taste and cook over moderate to hot heat until they have an even, golden glaze. Turn chestnuts carefully so that they do not break. Serve as garnish with meat or poultry.

CRANBERRY-APRICOT RELISH

4 cups (1 pound) raw cranberries
2 cups coarsely chopped dried apricots
1 cup coarsely chopped dried apples
½ cup golden raisins
1 tablespoon coarsely chopped preserved
    ginger
¼ cup whole filberts
1½ cups sugar or to taste
3½ cups water

Combine all ingredients. Bring to a boil. Lower heat and cook for 10 minutes or until cranberries have popped and are tender. Taste and add more sugar if desired. Store in refrigerator.

CRANBERRY-MINT RELISH

    1 pound fresh cranberries
    2 oranges
    ½ lemon
    6 large mint leaves
    1 cup sugar
      Dash cayenne
    ¼ teaspoon salt
    3 tablespoons brandy (optional)

Wash and chop cranberries fine. Squeeze juice from oranges and lemon. Remove membrane and chop peel fine. Chop mint leaves very fine. Add juice, peel and mint to cranberries along with sugar, cayenne, salt and brandy. Mix well and store in glass jar in refrigerator. Let stand at least overnight before serving.

MUSHROOM RELISH

½ pound fresh mushrooms, chopped fine
2 teaspoons minced parsley
2 teaspoons fresh lemon juice
2 tablespoons wine vinegar
2 tablespoons olive oil
   Salt and pepper to taste

Combine all ingredients and allow to stand overnight. Mixture will appear dry at first, but ample liquid will be drawn from mushrooms as they marinate. Serve with roast beef.

GOOSEBERRY SAUCE

1 can (16-oz.) gooseberries
½ cup sugar
1 tablespoon lemon juice
1 stick whole cinnamon
¼ teaspoon whole cloves

Combine all ingredients and cook over low heat 45 minutes, stirring frequently. Cool and store in refrigerator. Serve with meat or poultry.

PICKLED PRUNES

1 pound large prunes
2 cups water
½ cup cider vinegar
1 cup brown sugar
2 sticks cinnamon
8–10 cloves
4–5 allspice berries

Place prunes in a saucepan. Add all other ingredients. Simmer, covered, until prunes are puffy and tender (about 1 hour). Cool and refrigerate at least 2 days. Serve with roast goose, pork or ham.

PICKLED GRAPES

1 can (16-oz.) seedless grapes
¼ cup cider vinegar
¼ cup brown sugar
6 whole cloves
1 small stick cinnamon

Combine all ingredients and heat to boiling. Remove from stove and allow to cool. Refrigerate at least overnight. Serve with poultry or meat. Use as platter garnish in combination with pickled prunes.

RED & GREEN PEPPER RELISH

3 red bell peppers, chopped fine
3 green bell peppers, chopped fine
1 small onion, chopped fine
½ cup white vinegar
¼ cup sugar
⅓ cup olive oil
1 teaspoon salt
1 or 2 hot yellow chili peppers,
  chopped fine

Chop peppers and allow to stand 15 minutes. Drain accumulated juice. Add all other ingredients. Spoon into jar and refrigerate at least overnight before serving. Relish will keep well.

AVOCADO SALAD

(With Tomato Soup Dressing)

1 can (10¾-oz.) condensed tomato soup
½ cup salad oil
¾ cup vinegar
½ cup sugar
1 teaspoon dry mustard
1 teaspoon salt
1 teaspoon paprika
1 tablespoon Worcestershire sauce
2 tablespoons grated onion
    Ripe avocadoes

Combine all ingredients except avocadoes and beat well. Store in refrigerator for at least 6 hours. (Flavor improves with time.) Cut unpeeled avocadoes in half lengthwise (½ per person). Place on bed of lettuce. Remove seeds and fill cavities with dressing and serve.

CAULIFLOWER SLAW

1 large head cauliflower
1 small onion
2 large stalks celery
½ small bell pepper
¼ cup sliced pimento
½ to 1 cup sour cream
¼ cup sweet, creamy French dressing
Salt and pepper to taste

Slice all vegetables very thin, the thinner the better. Mix sour cream with French dressing. Stir into sliced vegetables. Add salt and pepper to taste. Chill before serving.

BUFFET FISH SALAD

Combine diced cold fillet of sole or any firm white fish with proportionate amounts of coarsely chopped pimento, minced celery, sliced white onions and bits of truffle or black olives. Mix with lemon mayonnaise. (Add 1 teaspoon fresh lemon juice to each ½ cup of mayonnaise.) Sprinkle with freshly ground black pepper and minced parsley.

RADISH SALAD

2 hard-cooked egg yolks
¾ cup sour cream
¼ cup mayonnaise
   Salt and pepper to taste
3 cups thinly sliced radishes
1 small head iceberg
   lettuce, shredded fine
   Parsley

Mash egg yolks until smooth. Combine with sour cream, mayonnaise, salt and pepper. Mix well and stir in radishes. Chill. Serve on individual nests of shredded lettuce. Garnish with small sprigs of parsley. Serve with roast beef.

GREEN BEAN & BEET SALAD

(With Parmesan Dressing)

1½–2 quarts mixed greens, iceberg
    lettuce, romaine, etc.
2 scallions, chopped fine
1 can (8-oz.) French style green beans
1 can (8-oz.) beets julienne
    Parmesan dressing

Tear greens into bite-size pieces. Refrigerate in a plastic bag or covered bowl for an hour or more. Add scallions. Toss with dressing. Add beans. Toss lightly. Add beets. Again toss lightly.

DRESSING:

1⅓ cups olive oil
½ cup red wine vinegar
¼ cup freshly grated Parmesan cheese
1 tablespoon sugar
1½ teaspoons salt
    Cracked pepper to taste
½ teaspoon dry mustard
1 small clove garlic

Combine all ingredients in a jar. Shake well and refrigerate. Remove garlic if dressing is kept more than 24 hours.

MUSHROOM SALAD

3 tablespoons olive oil
1 tablespoon lemon juice
  Cayenne pepper to taste
  Salt to taste
¼ teaspoon sugar
2 cups thinly sliced mushrooms
2 scallions, minced
1 tablespoon finely chopped pimento

Mix oil, lemon juice, seasonings and sugar. Add mushrooms and marinate for 1 hour. Stir in scallions and pimento. Serve in nest of shredded lettuce.

CARROT VICHYSSOISE

5 cups chicken broth
3 leeks, sliced thin
1 small onion, sliced thin
3 carrots, grated
4 large potatoes, grated
Salt and pepper to taste
1½ cups milk
1 cup heavy cream
Chives, minced

Combine chicken broth, leeks, onion, carrots and potatoes in heavy pan. Add salt and pepper and cook, covered, until vegetables are soft. Puree mixture in blender or put through sieve. Add milk and cream to puree and additional salt and pepper if necessary. Chill in refrigerator. Serve cold with minced chives as garnish.

CLEAR BORSCHT

2 small to medium-sized beets, peeled
   and coarsely grated
3 cans (14-oz. each) beef broth
1½ tablespoons lemon juice
1 egg white, lightly beaten
   Sour cream
   Parsley sprigs

Combine beets, beef broth and lemon juice in large pan. Stir in egg white. Simmer covered for ½ hour. Strain through a sieve lined with large (facial tissue-type) napkin. If soup cools return to heat for a few minutes. Garnish each serving with a dollop of thick sour cream and a small sprig of parsley.

PARSLEY CRACKERS

2 tablespoons butter
2 tablespoons parsley, minced
   Saltine crackers

Cream butter and add parsley gradually. Spread on crackers and cook under broiler until bubbly and crackers begin to brown. Serve with soup.

OYSTER CHOWDER

¼ cup finely chopped bell pepper
2 tablespoons finely chopped scallions
2 tablespoons finely chopped celery
2 tablespoons butter
12 ounces oysters in liquid
3½ cups cream (half-and-half for part of
    the cream)
1 tablespoon chopped pimento
1 tablespoon minced parsley
    Cayenne and salt to taste

Sauté bell pepper, scallions and celery in butter. Cook oysters in their liquid until edges curl. Scald cream. Add oysters and all other ingredients to cream and cook for 5 minutes. Do not boil. Serve with warm oyster crackers.

TURKEY-CORN CHOWDER

½ stick butter
3 medium-sized onions, coarsely chopped
3 large potatoes, diced
2 stalks celery, coarsely chopped
2 cups chicken stock
2 cans yellow, whole kernel corn
1 can yellow, cream-style corn
3 cups cooked cubed turkey
1 tablespoon chopped pimento
3 cups milk
1 cup cream
Salt and pepper to taste
Minced parsley

Sauté onion in butter in large, heavy pan. Add potatoes, celery and chicken stock. Simmer, covered, until vegetables are tender, not too soft. Add corn, turkey, pimento, milk, cream, salt and pepper. Simmer, covered, 5 minutes or until hot enough to serve. Garnish with minced parsley.

TOMATO BOUILLON

2 cups canned tomatoes
1 medium-sized onion, sliced
2 tablespoons butter
½ teaspoon salt
1 small clove garlic
2 cups strong beef stock
1 cup tomato juice
½ cup orange juice
1 small bay leaf
Salt and pepper to taste
Parsley
Whipped cream

Cook tomatoes, sliced onion, butter, salt and garlic in a covered pan over low heat for ½ hour. Then rub mixture through a fine sieve and return the puree to the pan. Add beef stock, tomato juice, orange juice and bay leaf. Simmer ½ hour. Discard bay leaf. Season with salt and pepper. Garnish with 1 tablespoon whipped cream and a small sprig of parsley. Serve hot or cold.

BAKED POTATO SOUP

2 large freshly baked potatoes
4 cups chicken broth
2 egg yolks
1 cup heavy cream
2 teaspoons minced parsley
2 teaspoons minced scallions
2 teaspoons sugar (This is essential.)
Salt and pepper to taste

While potatoes are still hot, remove flesh from the skins and press through a fine sieve. Combine with broth in a saucepan and bring to a low boil. Lower heat and simmer for 3 minutes. Remove from heat. Beat egg yolks with cream. Add to potato mixture along with remaining ingredients. Soup may be served hot or cold. When serving hot, do not allow soup to boil or it will curdle.

SWEET AND SOUR BRUSSELS SPROUTS

2 pounds Brussels sprouts
¼ cup sugar
⅔ cup white vinegar
⅓ cup water
½ teaspoon dry mustard
1 teaspoon salt
¼ teaspoon pepper
½ pound bacon, coarsely chopped
    and fried crisp
4 tablespoons bacon drippings

Cook sprouts in lightly salted water to cover until tender. Put all other ingredients except bacon into a jar fitted with a tight lid. Shake until well mixed. Pour into a saucepan and cook about 5 minutes stirring frequently until slightly thick. Pour over hot sprouts. Top with bacon bits and serve immediately.

CARROTS WITH ONION

6 large carrots
2 tablespoons butter
1 small onion, sliced thin
1 tablespoon sugar

1 teaspoon salt
2 teaspoons minced parsley
Cracked pepper to taste

Peel and slice carrots into thin sticks. Melt butter and add onion, sugar and salt. Cook over low heat until onion is transparent. Add parsley and carrots. Cook in ½ to 1 cup water, covered, until carrots are barely tender. During final minutes of cooking remove pan cover so that liquid is reduced. Add pepper and serve.

PUREED PEAS WITH MINT

2 packages frozen peas
10–12 sprigs fresh mint
4 tablespoons butter
Salt and pepper to taste

Cook peas with three mint sprigs in lightly salted water. When peas are tender, drain and place in blender along with 3 or 4 cooked mint leaves and butter. Puree mixture. Add salt and pepper to taste. Garnish roast platter with remaining sprigs of mint.

STUFFED EGGPLANT

2 medium-sized eggplants
Salt
Olive oil
2 medium-sized onions, sliced thin
2 large cloves garlic, minced
6 medium-sized, fresh mushrooms, sliced thin
3 tablespoons minced parsley
2 large tomatoes, peeled and chopped
½ teaspoon sugar
Salt and cracked pepper to taste

Cut eggplants lengthwise after removing stem. Scoop out flesh leaving a ½-inch shell and reserving pulp. Salt shell and set aside in a baking dish which has been greased generously with olive oil. Sauté onion and garlic in 1 tablespoon olive oil. Add diced eggplant pulp (almost 2½ cups). Add mushrooms. Cook 2 minutes. Add parsley, tomatoes, sugar, salt and pepper. Mix well and spoon into eggplant shells. Cover baking dish and place in 350° oven for about 1 hour or until eggplant shell is tender. Baste with pan juices. Cut shells in halves or thirds and serve warm or cold. A good buffet dish.

GREEN BEANS WITH MUSHROOMS

1 pound green beans, French cut
1 scallion, minced
1 tablespoon butter
½ pound small fresh mushrooms, sliced thin
   Salt and pepper to taste

In a covered pan cook beans and scallion in ½ cup water with a dash of salt until just tender. (Do not overcook.) Meanwhile sauté mushrooms in butter. Drain beans and add mushrooms, salt and pepper. Additional butter may be added to the vegetables if desired.

BEETS IN SHERRY

6–8 medium-sized beets
4 tablespoons butter
4 tablespoons honey
2 tablespoons orange juice
⅓ cup dry sherry

Cook beets, unpeeled, in salted water until tender. Combine butter, honey and orange juice. Simmer until well blended. Add sherry and set aside. When beets are done, peel, slice and add to the sauce. Heat for several minutes. Stir beets so that all the slices are covered with sauce. Serve hot.

MUSHROOMS IN SOUR CREAM

2 tablespoons finely chopped scallions
½ stick butter
1½ pounds whole button mushrooms or larger mushrooms, sliced lengthwise
2 tablespoons sour cream
2 teaspoons finely chopped pimento
Salt
Pepper

Sauté scallions in butter. Add mushrooms and cook until barely tender. Stir in sour cream and pimento and cook over low heat until warm enough to serve. Do not cook over high heat. Season to taste and serve.

LETTUCE IN SOUR CREAM

3 tablespoons butter
2 tablespoons flour
1 cup chicken stock
   Salt and pepper to taste
2 heads iceberg lettuce, washed,
   dried and shredded
1 cup sour cream
1 tablespoon cider vinegar
2 tablespoons capers, rinsed
1 tablespoon chopped pimento

In a heavy skillet melt the butter and blend in flour. Stir constantly until mixture bubbles. Stir in stock and season with salt and pepper. Reserve ½ cup of the shredded lettuce and add the rest to the sauce in the skillet. Scald sour cream and combine with vinegar and capers. Add to lettuce. Cover tightly and simmer gently for 10 minutes. Add reserved lettuce and pimento and serve immediately.

CREAMED ONIONS WITH PEPPERS

24 small white onions
2 tablespoons butter
2 tablespoons flour
1 cup light cream
1 teaspoon chili powder
½ teaspoon salt
½ teaspoon coarsely ground pepper
1 large bell pepper, sliced thin
1 tablespoon chopped pimento

Peel onions and cook in salted boiling water until just tender. In a saucepan over low heat blend butter and flour together. Add cream gradually, stirring constantly until mixture thickens. Add chili powder and salt. Sauté sliced pepper in butter until just tender. Drain onions very well and add them to the sauce along with the peppers and pimento. Heat well, but do not boil. Serve.

MASHED APPLESAUCE-POTATOES

Mix equal parts of hot mashed potatoes with hot applesauce. Season with sugar, salt, pepper and dash of vinegar (optional) to taste. Top with melted butter. Serve with roast goose or baked ham.

POTATO SOUFFLÉ

2 cups thick mashed potatoes
½ cup heavy cream
1 teaspoon salt
¼ to ½ teaspoon ground pepper
⅛ teaspoon nutmeg
2 tablespoons grated Parmesan cheese
3 egg yolks, beaten
4 egg whites, beaten (but not too dry)

Combine potatoes, cream, salt, pepper and nutmeg and cook over low heat until very hot, being careful not to scorch mixture. Remove from heat and mix in egg yolks one third at a time, beating well after each addition. Cool and then fold in egg whites. Fill a buttered soufflé or baking dish three-fourths full and bake in 375° oven until mixture puffs and is lightly browned (30–35 minutes).

CELERY WITH ALMONDS

4 cups sliced celery stalks
4 tablespoons butter
1 tablespoon finely chopped chives
2 tablespoons grated onion
1½ tablespoons flour

1 cup cream
½ cup chicken bouillon
1 cup almonds, blanched,
   shredded, toasted
Salt and pepper to taste

Put celery and butter into saucepan. Cover and cook gently until celery slices are tender. Add chives and onion and stir well. Sprinkle flour over celery and stir thoroughly. Add cream and bouillon slowly stirring constantly until sauce thickens. Boil for 1 minute stirring constantly. Stir in almonds. Add salt and pepper to taste.

BRAISED CHESTNUTS

2 pounds chestnuts, peeled
   Chicken stock
   Ground pepper and salt to taste
2 tablespoons butter

To peel chestnuts slit each shell and boil in water to cover for 20 minutes. Drain and cool. Peel off shells and place chestnuts in a saucepan. Add stock to a depth of 1 inch. Cover, bring to a boil, reduce heat and simmer until just tender (10 to 15 minutes). Stir in butter and seasoning.

SPINACH RING WITH CREAMED CHESTNUTS

4 pounds spinach
1 teaspoon grated onion
1/8 teaspoon nutmeg
   Salt and pepper to taste
3 egg whites

2 cups whole chestnuts
2 tablespoons butter
2½ tablespoons flour
1½-2 cups milk
   Salt and pepper to taste

Cook spinach and drain very thoroughly. Chop coarsely and combine with onion, nutmeg, salt and pepper. Mix well. Fold in stiffly beaten egg whites and spoon into a buttered ring mold. Place mold in a shallow pan of hot water and bake covered with waxed paper at 400° for 10 minutes. Reduce heat to 350° and continue baking 30 minutes. Meanwhile pierce chestnuts with a sharp knife and boil until tender. Drain. Peel chestnuts while hot. In a saucepan melt butter and blend in flour. Stirring constantly, add 1½ cups milk. Cook until thickened. Add more milk if sauce is too thick. Season and stir in chestnuts. Unmold spinach and spoon creamed chestnuts into the center of the ring.

SWEET POTATOES WITH BOURBON & WALNUTS

4½ pounds sweet potatoes or yams
1½ sticks butter, melted
⅓ to ½ cup bourbon
½ teaspoon salt
2 tablespoons butter
⅓ cup brown sugar, firmly packed
½ cup coarsely chopped walnuts

Cook sweet potatoes in lightly salted water until soft. Remove skins. Beat potatoes in mixer until smooth. Heat melted butter, bourbon and salt until hot (not boiling) and beat into potatoes. Spoon mixture into a well-buttered 6-cup baking dish, dot with 2 tablespoons butter and top with brown sugar and walnuts. Bake in 350° oven 20 minutes.

YAMS WITH APPLES

3 large yams
3 large apples, peeled, sliced thin
Sugar
Ground cloves

Ground cinnamon
Butter

Cook yams until tender in boiling salted water to cover. Peel yams and cut into ½ inch-thick slices. Place a layer of yams in the bottom of a buttered baking dish, sprinkle lightly with sugar and dot with butter. Add a layer of apples, sprinkle with sugar and dot with butter. Repeat layers. Top with sprinkling of ground cloves and cinnamon. Cover and bake in 350° oven 30 to 40 minutes or until apples are tender.

MASHED TURNIPS

4 large turnips (about 2 pounds)
1 large baking potato
1 teaspoon salt
2 tablespoons butter
Cracked pepper to taste

Peel and cut up turnips and potato. Cover with water and 1 teaspoon salt. Cook, covered, until tender. Drain thoroughly and mash. Add butter and pepper. Serve hot. To keep warm, spoon into casserole, dot with additional butter, cover and place in 250° oven until ready to serve.

BROCCOLI WITH PIMENTO SAUCE

    2 pounds broccoli
    2 tablespoons butter
    ½ cup sliced green onions
    ¼ cup chopped and drained pimento
    1 teaspoon grated lemon rind
    2 tablespoons lemon juice
      Salt and pepper to taste

After trimming leaves and tough portions from broccoli, split stalks in half or quarters and cook in salted water until barely tender. Meanwhile sauté onions in butter. Remove from heat and stir in remaining ingredients. Place thoroughly drained broccoli in a serving dish and pour pimento mixture over the top.

ZUCCHINI SAUTÉ

    1 pound fresh, crisp zucchini,
        coarsely grated
    1 tablespoon butter
      Salt and pepper to taste

Place zucchini and butter in a heavy skillet. Cook over medium to high heat until zucchini is barely tender. It should be slightly crisp. Add salt and pepper to taste.

RICE-CORN CASSEROLE

2 cups cooked rice
2 tablespoons minced onion
2 tablespoons minced bell pepper
2 tablespoons butter
1 can (17-oz.) white cream-style corn
1 cup grated Cheddar cheese
2 eggs, well beaten
1½ tablespoons chopped pimento
Salt and pepper to taste
⅓ cup grated Cheddar cheese

While rice is cooking, sauté onion and bell pepper in butter. Remove from heat and allow to cool for 5 minutes. Add rice and all other ingredients except ⅓ cup grated cheese. Mix well and spoon into buttered casserole or baking dish. Top with remaining cheese. Bake in 375° oven until bubbly and cheese is melted (about 15 minutes).

MIXED VEGETABLES

¾ pound fresh string beans, julienne
1 package frozen baby lima beans
1 large bell pepper, julienne
1 package frozen petits pois
   Salt
   Coarse ground pepper
2 tablespoons butter, melted
⅔ cup heavy cream, slightly whipped
1 tablespoon mayonnaise

Cook vegetables separately in salted boiling water. Meanwhile, melt butter, mix cream with mayonnaise and warm a deep baking dish. When vegetables are tender, drain and season to taste with salt and pepper. Working quickly, so that vegetables do not cool, place string beans on bottom of baking dish, cover with lima beans followed by peppers and finally the peas. Dribble butter over all and top with cream-mayonnaise mixture. Garnish with strips of pimento, place under a slow broiler for 3 or 4 minutes. Serve immediately.

OTHER COOKBOOKS WRITTEN BY
JUNE DUTTON AND PUBLISHED BY
DETERMINED PRODUCTIONS, INC. ARE:

HORS D'OEUVRE
BOOZE
SMÖRGÅSBORD
COCINA MEXICANA
MANGIARE ALLA ITALIANA
PEANUTS COOKBOOK
PEANUTS LUNCH BAG COOKBOOK

OTHER DETERMINED PRODUCTIONS
BOOKS ILLUSTRATED BY
BRUCE BUTTE ARE:

COCINA MEXICANA
PACIFIC ISLANDS COOKBOOK